Happiness Starts Here

by Robert D. Isett, PhD

Happiness Starts Here

Robert D. Isett, PhD

Happiness Starts Here © by Robert D. Isett PhD

This book was printed in the United States of America.

ISBN: 978-0-9845008-3-3

Additional copies of this book are available from Amazon.com, Create Space, and other retail outlets.

Website: www.thinkrightfeelright.net

email: thinkrightfeelright1@yahoo.com

Dear Parents, Teachers and Counselors,

We know that good emotional health requires a sound foundation. Behavioral education strengthens this foundation by improving our coping abilities, positivity, and self-confidence. *Happiness Start Here* creates this opportunity for young minds.

Happiness Starts Here helps children master essential concepts and behavioral tools for emotional health. Aided by age-appropriate practical examples, illustrations and exercises, young readers gain important knowledge about feelings and emotions as well as core skills for emotional health and happiness.

Happiness Starts Here is an important educational resource in the home and in the classroom.

Now let's get started on some real happiness wizardry here at The Happiness Academy. You are about to become a wizard at understanding what *emotions* are, what causes them, and what makes them better. You will become the master of how you feel. And, you will become the master of your happiness. Are you ready?

WHAT ARE EMOTIONS?

When Winnie and I talk about emotions and feelings, we are usually talking about the same thing. What do these words mean to you? If you think you know what a feeling is, write your answer:

_____

_____

_____

_____

OK, we know that this is not an easy question. As Winnie and I discovered, most people have trouble describing what emotions are or the best ways to fix them. Without this knowledge, they have difficulty holding on to happiness. But don't worry, we will make sure that you gain the answers you need to master your emotions and happiness. Let' get started!

Emotions are feelings. Emotions are the feelings we get when we are happy, or sad, or excited. We *feel* emotions and that's why we refer to them sometimes as feelings. We feel emotions as sensations in certain areas of our body. We can notice them when we are excited, sad or fearful. Different emotions can cause different sensations. These

sensations help us to recognize them. For example, when we are afraid, we feel our heart racing or notice that we are breathing faster. We feel certain sensations when we are sad or about to cry. What sensations do you notice when you are frightened?

_____

_____

_____

_____

Emotions are important signals for happiness. When you are really happy, notice how good you feel. These feelings let you know you are in a good place. When you are scared or very sad, you get these signals that let you know you are not in a good place and that you probably need to change direction.

If you learn to use *emotional signals* well, you will have a better aim on happiness. Your feelings help you to see when you are unhappy so you can do something about it. They point out where you find happiness, so you can find it again.

Emotional signals also let others know how we feel so they can help too. Our faces (facial expressions), our body language, and our words send these signals.

There are many things that the brain and body do to produce these signals, but right now Winnie and I want to talk to you about what our faces do.

Faces say a lot about emotion. Our facial expressions signal others about how we feel. They let others know that we are happy, bored, or upset about something. What does this student's face say to you? When we pay close attention to facial expressions, we are able to help each other to stay on the road to happiness.

How does your face show emotion? If you have a mirror handy, let's make some faces and find out. While looking in the mirror, make the face that you make when you are really happy. Notice how you change your expression. What changes do you see around your mouth, your eyes? How wide is your smile?

OK, now look puzzled. Notice how your face changes when you look puzzled. Did you wrinkle your brow? Do you see any other changes in your expression? Your mouth maybe? Your face changes as you express different emotions. We acquire many different facial expressions to show how we feel. Let's do one more: Show the mirror your sad face. Excellent, but Winnie and I like your happy face much, much better!

While we are discussing faces and the ways faces communicate emotions, please look over the emoji faces we picked out for you. What feelings do these faces express? Write your answers above the emojis.

_____   _____   _____   _____

Notice the differences in the emoji faces. These differences help you to figure out their emotions. BTW, we love it when you feel the way the emoji on the right does!

Our *body language sends emotional signals.* Body language refers to the way we use our body to reveal feelings. We use body language, like waves, smiles, frowns, crossed arms, thumbs up or down, to send messages to others about our feelings. These gestures help others to recognize the way we feel. A clenched fist is a warning sign. Thumbs up signals that things are good. We learn many body signals to express emotion.

Look at these two emojis. They have their hands around each other. What does their body language tell you about how they feel toward each other? You got it! These emojis really like each other.

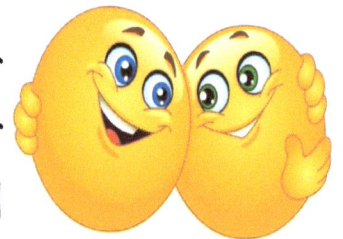

Now, look again at this emoji with the v-shaped hands under his chin. The body language increases the amount of happiness shown in the emoji drawing. Body language can tell us a lot about how someone feels.

Let's look at *your* body language next. What body language do you use to show that you are really frustrated? Notice your hands. What are your hands doing? What about your face? Did you change your facial expression?

What would your body look like if you just found out you won a million dollars? Would you be jumping up and down with joy? If so, your body language would be showing the world how happy you are!

Our words are important emotional signals, too. Words are one of the best ways we have to help each other understand our feelings. Words express our joys and our sorrows. Through our words, we let others know what we like and what we don't like, what we need and don't need, and much, much more. Our words help us to make things better. Talking about feelings is one of the best ways to make things better. As happiness wizards, we learn to listen to our feelings and express them in words. When we are aware of our feelings and we communicate them well, we are able to understand each other better. We give happiness a better chance when we learn how to express our feelings in words. Practice helps.

Here is a practice opportunity for you: A friend makes fun of the new coat that you received for your birthday. You feel hurt by what they said. Think carefully about the words you would choose to let your friend know how you feel. What might you say? Please be sure to begin with the words, "I feel ... ." Write the words you chose below:

_____

_____

_____

_____

_____

Here is another practice situation to help you express feelings: Suppose you forgot that today was your mother's birthday. How would you express your feelings?

I'm Sorry!

_____

_____

_____

_____

Emotional signals protect us. Words, facial expressions and other body language let others know about our *boundaries.* Boundaries are very important; they help to define who we are. They clarify what we like and what we don't like. When we say *"no"* or give a *"thumbs down gesture,"* for example, we are expressing a boundary that says we don't like something. Emotional signals protect our boundaries and our happiness. Use them to protect yourself.

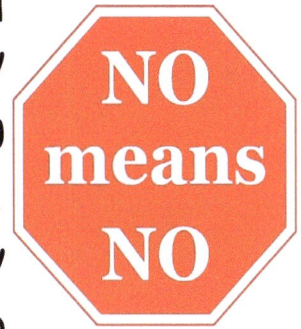

Remember, your feelings and emotions are signals that help you see and adjust to the world around you. Your feelings, facial expressions, body language, and words are signals that help guide your life and the lives of others toward happiness. Listen to these signals. Express your feelings in words. They help your happiness and they protect you.

WHAT CAUSES EMOTION?

If you know what causes emotion, you may already be a happiness wizard. If you are not sure, we can help. Many people think that the world around them causes their happiness or their unhappiness. They have the idea that "things" cause people to feel good or bad.

When they feel sad, they blame "things" for making them feel sad. They think that "things," like a new cell phone or a trip to Disney World, bring happiness. But, that is not exactly the way feelings work, and that is not the way happiness works.

It is true that we connect "things" like a new coat, or a *new cell phone*, or a family vacation with happiness. Our minds tell us that we will be happier if we get the new coat, the new cell phone, or the vacation. We also connect events with unhappiness. For example, we get angry or upset because we didn't get to go on vacation or unhappy because the new coat was too small. "Things" often appear to be the cause of our happiness or unhappiness, but are they?

Although it may seem otherwise, "things" don't really cause emotions. Suppose you are *sad* because your cat, Sassafras, is missing. But then you find her hiding in the clothes hamper. Now, you feel *happy* again. Did Sassafras make you feel this way?

No, actually you did. To be more precise, your *thoughts* did. Your thoughts caused these feelings, not Sassafras. Your thoughts made you feel upset when you couldn't find Sassafras. Your thoughts made you happy again after you found her. Your thoughts stirred these feelings of unhappiness and happiness.

What do we mean by *thoughts?* We mean the ideas you get in your mind when you think about something. We call these ideas, *thoughts.* For example, thoughts are the images you have or words you say to yourself when you think about seeing a movie, a new coat, raking leaves or broccoli. Become aware of the thoughts that stir your emotions. These thoughts direct your feelings, and these thoughts direct your happiness.

People react differently to the same thing because of the various ways they learn to think about something. Randy pushes his plate away whenever he sees broccoli on it. That's because Randy thinks that broccoli tastes awful. Brady, his younger brother, always asks for more broccoli. Brady loves it. He thinks broccoli tastes delicious. Because he thinks this way, he gets in trouble sometimes because he tries to steal it from Randy.

Adele is supposed to rake the leaves after school today. She learns that heavy rainfall is expected all day. She is delighted. Adele hates raking leaves so she is happy to get out of raking them. Her younger sister, Reagan, is sad. Reagan is very disappointed that she won't get to play in the leaves today while her sister rakes them. The girls feel very differently about this situation because their thoughts are very different. Our thoughts often cause us to feel and react in very different ways.

Your friend backs away when you try to show him your wonderful pet snake, Flicker. What emotional signal is he sending you? What do you suppose he *thinks* about Flicker? If you guessed that he thinks Flicker might bite him, you are right. Fearful thoughts make us feel afraid and pull back. They cause us to act fearfully. If these thoughts are true, they help us to avoid danger. If they are false, they just get in the way of happiness.

Thoughts cause happiness and unhappiness. Notice that the way we think about something stirs up feelings. Adele "hates raking leaves." Because she thinks this way, she causes herself to strongly dislike raking them. If we have negative thoughts about pet snakes or broccoli or sleeping in the dark, we start to feel bad when we see or even think about these things. Negative thoughts weaken happiness. They take happiness away.

The reverse is true for positive thoughts. For instance, if you love chocolate chip cookies, you feel delight when you think about them, or you find the chance to eat one as it comes out of the oven still warm!

Reagan not only loves to play in the leaves, she even loves to think about playing in them. Positive thoughts strengthen happiness. Positive thoughts bring us more happiness.

Remember, your *thoughts*, not things or the world around you, make you feel the way you feel. You cause the way you feel, so you can always do something about it. You can always change the way you think and improve happiness.

HOW TO FIX EMOTIONS AND HAPPINESS

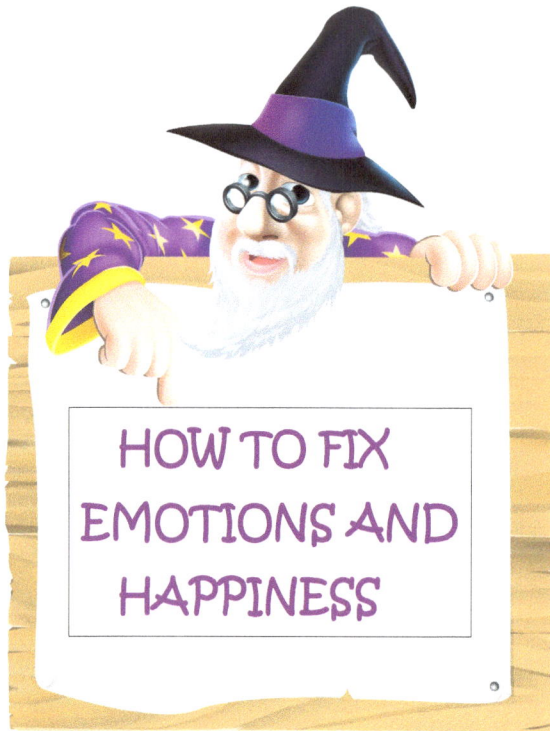

Positive thoughts are a good choice for happiness. Troublesome thoughts (like worry, anger, sadness) are not. As happiness wizards discover, thoughts have a big influence on happiness. When we spend a lot of time worrying about things, feeling sad, or picking out things we don't like about ourselves or the world around us, we push happiness away. The more negative we are, the more stuck we get in unhappiness.

Negative thinking makes us unhappy. Negative thinking just brings us down. Too much of it can make us anxious or depressed. Because negative thinking hurts happiness and often leads to emotional problems, this behavior is a poor choice.

To make happiness grow, we learn to use positive thoughts rather than negative ones. By thinking well, we make our world better. We feel better. We are more fun to be around. And, we have more energy to accomplish things and to enjoy life. Negative thoughts waste energy and happiness. Positive thinking increases both. Positive thinking is definitely the best choice for happiness.

Maybe you suspect that changing your thoughts will be difficult. Actually, it isn't. You do it all the time. You constantly learn and build new thoughts about your world. It is better and easier to change your thinking than to use thoughts that don't work well. You don't have to wait for "things" to change for you to be happy. *You already have the green light.* You can change your thinking and move forward. That's what happiness wizards do!

So, how can you get better at changing the way you think? First, pay close attention to your feelings. Feelings offer important clues. Feelings help you to notice the thoughts and behaviors that are good for you and ones that cause trouble. Feelings help guide you.

Your emotions suggest ideas for adding more goodness and happiness to life. For example, maybe you *notice how good you feel after you help someone.* Your feelings let you know that you feel especially good when you help someone or *think* about being helpful. So, if you keep helpfulness in your thoughts, you add happiness to your world.

Here is another example of how feelings can help us to find positive thgoughts. Suppose that you have a cat named Ruby. You love everything about her. You love the way she looks. You love to hold her, and you love to play with her. *You think Ruby is absolutely terrific.*

When you feel happy about Ruby, notice your thinking. What are you saying to yourself? You think she is wonderful and, because you do, you love her to pieces. These are the kind of thoughts that create happiness.

So, to master your own happiness, follow these three important steps:

1) Find positive thoughts.
2) Increase positive thinking.
3) Fix thoughts that hurt happiness.

As happiness wizards, we know the importance of practice. We will go over each of these steps, and allow you to practice them, so you can do them on your own.

Step One: Find positive thoughts. Winnie asked me to give you some examples of my positive thoughts. Here are a few of them: I love to help people. I have a wonderful family. Golden sunlight is really beautiful. Collecting old toy trains is so much fun.

OK, Now you try it! Search your mind for positive thoughts as you answer these questions:

Think positive!

When do I feel most happy? _____
_____
_____
_____
_____

What makes me laugh? _____
_____
_____
_____
_____

What do I love? _____

_____

_____

_____

_____

What makes the world a better place? _____

_____

_____

_____

_____

What really excites me? _____

_____

_____

_____

_____

If you found five positive thoughts, nice work! Please continue reading. If you had trouble finding positive thoughts, please search a little while longer. Remember to ask for help if you need it.

This first step helps you to find your positive thoughts. Practice bringing these good thoughts to your attention. Notice that positive thoughts work even when you are not around the "things" that you are happy about. Since you can think these thoughts whenever you wish, you can improve happiness whenever you want to just by having these thoughts. Turn on your positive thinking and you will feel happier. Learn to focus on positive thoughts every day. This habit will really help you to keep happiness around.

Step Two: Increase positive thinking. Positive thinking pays off. When you fill your mind with good thoughts, you feel more energy, and you feel happier. To excel at happiness, find and use positive thoughts every day.

Positive thoughts are all around you. There are millions of things to be grateful for, so you have a very long list of *grateful thoughts* to choose from. The list is just as long for other positive thoughts: *beautiful thoughts, fun thoughts, amazing thoughts, peaceful thoughts, helpful thoughts, exciting* thoughts, and so on. You have endless ways to gain more happiness.

Positive thinking builds happiness. Encourage positive thinking by looking for positive ways to view life. By encouraging your mind to think positively, you put yourself in charge of happiness.

You can create new positive thoughts, anywhere, anytime, about almost anything. As an example, you can form a new positive thought right now by thinking, "I really like learning about positive thinking. I can't wait to use it more."

You can create positive thoughts about things that happened as well as things that may never happen. For example, you could think, "It's fun to think about having a twin sister." Every time you create one of these good thoughts, you improve your outlook on your world.

Positive thinking brings you and the world around you greater joy.

Now, for practice, we would like you to come up with three *new* thoughts that lift your happiness. Write your thoughts below:

1) Positive Thought:_____

_____

_____

_____

2) Positive Thought:_____

_____

_____

_____

3) Positive Thought:_____

_____

_____

_____

Positive thoughts work well, but they only work well if you remember to use them. So, your job is to use them often. New positive thoughts give you more ways to enjoy life. New or old though, positive thoughts will lift happiness over and over again. How do you increase positive thinking? First, make a plan.

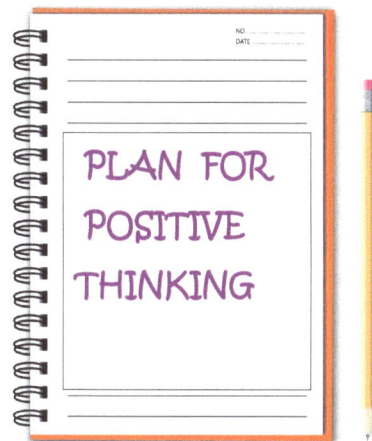

The best way to change a behavior, like positive thinking, is to start with a good plan. A good plan for changing behavior *always* includes:

1) the behavior you wish to master

2) what you will do to master this behavior

3) a way to make sure you follow your plan

Let's take Denzel as an example. He wants to increase positive thinking so he can be happier. To help him reach his goal, he needs to create a good plan. He decides he will think more often about some of the favorite things in his life (his dog named Hollyberry, his best friend Darius, summer vacations with his family, and *ice skating with Makayla*, his older sister).

He realizes practice is important. He decides he will practice this thinking at least five times every day during the week. Denzel uses familiar daily activities as reminders: He will practice positive thinking when he brushes his teeth in the morning, when he leaves for school, during lunch break, while returning home from school, and after dinner. Each evening before going to bed, he will ask himself if he remembered to practice as he planned. If he forgets, he will practice these thoughts before going to sleep.

Denzel has a good plan, but how long should he continue with it? He wants to make certain this new behavior becomes a habit. So, Denzel will stick with his plan until he can bring these positive thoughts to his mind easily. When he is able to think this way, he has developed a habit.

Denzel can design many other plans to build positive thinking and happiness. For example, he could decide to use positive thinking whenever he notices that he is feeling down. When he feels down he will tell himself, "I don't have to continue to feel this way. Better thinking will help." At the end of the day, he will check to see if he followed his plan. Denzel continues with the plan until this new thinking becomes a habit.

Positive thoughts do more than improve happiness. They reinforce (strengthen) behavior. If Nazia decides to tell herself good things about going to school, this will increase her interest in school and make school more enjoyable. Positive thoughts reinforce behavior and happiness

Positive thinking improves the way we feel *and* the way we behave. For example, love for nature lifts our spirits and motivates us to be more caring about the world around us. Positive thoughts that place value on helping others encourage us to be more helpful. Positive thinking makes the world a better place.

Sabrina decides to use positive thinking to improve her tennis game and her happiness. Here is Sabrina's problem: She moves her head too much while hitting the tennis ball, which causes her to miss a lot. She becomes frustrated and loses concentration. Her happiness goes away. So, she creates a plan.

Her plan is to compliment herself every time she holds her head still while hitting the ball. Compliments are positive thoughts that reinforce behavior. They help her to keep her head still. Positive thinking helps Sabrina to hit better shots, stay focused, and enjoy playing tennis.

The following exercise will help you build more positive thinking: Think about the kind of positive thinking that you would like to increase. After you have an idea, we would like you to design a plan that helps you achieve this goal. Answering each of the questions below will help you to design a good plan:

1) What positive thought(s) do you wish to have?

_____
_____
_____
_____

2) How often will you practice this behavior, and what reminders will you use? _____

_____
_____
_____
_____
_____
_____
_____

3) What will you do if you forgot to follow your plan? _____

_____

_____

_____

_____

4) How will you know that you met your goal?_____

_____

_____

_____

_____

Step 3) Fix Negative Thinking. Pay attention to your feelings. If you notice that you feel afraid of pet snakes, for instance, these feelings are telling you that you have scary thoughts about pet snakes. Realize that because you tell yourself these scary thoughts, you continue to make yourself afraid. To get over this fear, you choose a different way of thinking, for example a more relaxing thought. You decide to tell yourself, *"Pet snakes are actually pretty friendly little creatures. They won't really hurt me."* Practice this new way of thinking, and you learn to get over this fear.

If you find that you worry too much, you find your worry thoughts and fix them. Let's say you discover that you worry that you are too tall or that your hands are too small. You realize that such worries are a waste of time and happiness. Instead of making yourself feel bad about your body, you decide to think this way: *"This is my body and it's fine the way it is. If I get rid of these troublesome thoughts, pretty soon I will feel much better."*

Suppose you are someone who worries about grades all the time. You see that these worries bring you down. Rather than worry so much, you decide to use positive thinking. Your new thoughts are, *"I will just concentrate on doing the best I can with my schoolwork. If I need to work a little harder or get extra help, I will."* Now, with this better way of thinking, you have fewer worries, better happiness, and more energy to get things done.

Sara is 11 years old. She goes out of her way to make friends with a group of girls at school, but they don't include her very often. She has tried to talk to them about this problem, but still they have not been very friendly. Sara does not understand why they treat her this way. She continues to be upset because they usually don't include her. What is she to do?

Even if our best efforts to change problems in the world around us fail, we can always fix the way we feel by fixing our thoughts. *Sara can think, "These girls don't act like good friends. I tried my best to be friends with them, and they still aren't very nice to me. I will stop getting myself upset about them, and I will look for other friends who are nicer."* Her new thoughts allow her to move forward. By getting rid of her negative thoughts, and changing direction, Sara feels better and looks for better friends.

We know that kids encounter problems while on the internet, like *cyberbullying*. Harper ran into this problem: Harper stays in touch with her friends almost every day through the internet. Lately, however, a few of these "friends" started leaving very negative comments about her.

Harper is very hurt by this. She can't understand why friends would treat her like this, or what she might have done to cause this problem. When she asks them about it, they ignore her and leave more negative comments.

After talking to her parents and her teacher at school about the situation, Harper realizes that she is being bullied by these kids. So, she decides to stop all communications with them. From now on, she will only pick friends who treat her, and each other, with respect. These new thoughts help Harper to feel better, create stronger boundaries, and end the cyberbullying problem.

Great work! You have learned a great deal about how emotions work and about how to improve happiness. You are almost there. Winnie and I have only one more exercise for you. We would like you to help Aaron fix his negative thinking.

Here is what happened: Aaron allowed Jake, his younger brother, to borrow his new cell phone. Now the camera on his cell phone doesn't work properly. Jake says that he didn't do anything to the camera. Aaron *has been angry* and upset ever since this happened.

What can Aaron do to make things better? How can he fix his troublesome thinking? What should Aaron do to help avoid this problem in the future? What should he say to Jake? Name three steps that Aaron could take:

1) _____

_____

_____

_____

2) _____

_____

_____

_____

3) _____

_____

_____

_____

Remember, your thoughts create your happiness and unhappiness. It is a good idea to get rid of thoughts that create trouble, and replace them with positive thoughts. Make a plan and be sure to follow it. Positive thinking is what happiness wizards do every day. Choose positive thoughts. Positive thoughts are free. Every time you use them happiness comes for free.

Wow! Our happiness meter indicates that you have done quite well here at the Happiness Academy. We know that you worked hard. You learned about emotions and discovered new ways to improve happiness. Please continue to practice what you have learned with us so you add more and more happiness to your life every day.

HAPPINESS WIZARD

Winnie and I are very happy that we had the opportunity to work with you at the Happiness Academy. And now, seeing that you have completed all of the required studies for Happiness Wizardry, and that you have mastered the skills pertaining thereto, with the powers and authorities vested in us, we officially and most happily inform you that you are now a Happiness Wizard. In recognition of your fine work, we wish to present you with this Certificate of Achievement. Please be sure to sign your name on this certificate.

CONGRATULATIONS!

Certificate of Achievement
of
Agriculture and Applied Science

Name:

having successfully completed the studies prescribed for the Curriculum in

HAPPINESS WIZARDRY

and having been recommended by the faculty is, by the State Board
of Higher Education, conferred the degree of

HAPPINESS WIZARD

December, 2011

Signature *Willhelmus Wizard*

Thank you for coming to learn with us at the Happiness Academy. We loved having you here.

If you would like to share any comments or suggestions about your experience with *Happiness Starts Here*, we would love to hear from you. You can email us at: thinkrightfeelright1@yahoo.com. You can also contact us through our website: www.thinkrightfeelright.net.

Winnie and I have just begun work on a new project: "Building Confidence and Self-Esteem." We think you might really like it. We hope to see you again.

Wishing you much happiness,

Willie and Winnie

Acknowledgments

Completed works often rest upon the shoulders of many. This is certainly true with *Happiness Starts Here.* I am privileged to know many kind and capable people who helped along the way. I wish to acknowledge:

Harv Martens, Maryann Roszkowski, William Rozycki, and Ryan Reidy: Thank you for your well-wishes, support and timely help

Linda Raitt, Pam Fisher and Janet Querner: I am deeply grateful for the generous help each of you gave. Your thoughtful reviews, ideas and expert editorial assistance greatly improved the final product.

Pam Lione: Accomplished writer and author, literary adviser, and very good soul. Thank you for your generous help and friendship.

Matthew Querner: All around wonderful young man. Thank you for giving me the inspiration to write this book during our summer vacation with you several years ago.

Karin Isett: My exceptional, loving, life partner, and my nuts and bolts editor-in-chief. Your help was invaluable. No man could be more fortunate.

David, Ben, Jaclyn, and Brian Isett, and Sharon Spillman: Thank you for your loving support and always being there.

www.ingramcontent.com/pod-product-compliance
Lightning Source LLC
Chambersburg PA
CBHW060832270326
41933CB00002B/63